SUDEK

sonja bullaty

Clarkson N. Potter, Inc. / Publishers NEW YORK

DISTRIBUTED BY CROWN PUBLISHERS, INC.

ACKNOWLEDGEMENTS

My most grateful thanks to Dr. Brumlik for sharing some of his early reminiscences of Sudek with me and for letting me choose several photographs from his collection to be included in this book: Plates 12, 24, 26, 44, 74, 76; and to Anna Farova for so generously participating in this tribute to our mutual friend.

Thanks also to Grace Mayer and Steve Zane for their help and advice; to Eva Fukova for letting me read and use part of the manuscript of the memoirs of her late husband Vladimir Fuka; and to my friends for their encouragement and help.

My very special gratitude to Woody Eitel for believing in this book from the start and for convincing me that I could do it; and of course to Angelo Lomeo, my husband, whose many ideas are part of this book and without whose patience and sense of humor I could never have finished this project.

I would also like to thank the following whose writing about Sudek was helpful to me in the preparation of this book: Jan Rezac, Lubomir Linhart, Antonin Dufek, Marie Kulijevycova, Daniela Mrazkova, Zdenek Kirschner, Petr Tausk, Allan Porter, James Sage, Ruth Spencer, Charles Sawyer, and Michael Edelson.

SUDEK
has been designed by Babs Beresford of New York.
The plates have been printed in sheet-fed gravure
and the text has been printed in sheet-fed offset
by Roto/Sadag, S.A., Geneva, Switzerland.
It has been set in Linotype Palatino
by The Hallmark Press, New York.
The book was bound by Reliure Veihl, S.A., Geneva, Switzerland.

THIS IS A RUGGLES DE LATOUR, INC. BOOK
NEW YORK

Published simultaneously in Canada by General Publishing Company Limited
First edition
Printed in Switzerland

Library of Congress Cataloging in Publication Data

Sudek, Josef, 1896–1976.
Sudek. 1. Sudek, Josef, 1896–1976. 2. Photography, Artistic. 3. Photographers—Czechoslovakia—Prague—Biography. I. Bullaty, Sonja.
TR140.S737A34 1978 779'.092'4 [B] 78-17573 ISBN 0-517-53294-8

CONTENTS

To Sudek,
and to the young at any age
who continue the search
for truth and beauty
. . . there is music . . .

INTRODUCTION

by Anna Farova

Photography, as no other art form, is tied to reality in such a way that without it, photography cannot even exist. A photographer must project his own personal experiences and his own attitude toward life if he wants to leave behind him a unique and universal message.

From the beginning Sudek searched for his own expression although he did not hesitate to accept the most varied artistic influences. He realized at once that photography was an independent means of expression, embodying a new theory of art not then accepted in Europe. Even as he studied photography in the twenties with the somewhat old-fashioned professor Karel Novak of the School of Graphic Arts in Prague (who taught in the official style of the Viennese school), even then he looked for his own road. Trends outside the curriculum influenced him; he made contacts with amateur photographers and met and debated with his friend Jaromir Funke, the only professional photographer in his life.

Funke was about the same age as Sudek and came from the same region of the country. He had studied law, medicine, and philosophy, but in the twenties he devoted himself completely to photography. A well-read and informed man, it was Funke's desire to elevate photography to a real and accepted art form without the involvement of the painterly tradition. Early on he became the avant-garde leader of modern photography in Czechoslovakia. Sudek, on the other hand, was intuitive and emotional, but with absolute vision. His dis-coveries in photography were spontaneous and not premeditated. He kept discovering in photography what was essential and unique for his expression, and he separated this from the accidental. His dedication to photography was as intense as to any religious order or newly wed wife.

Painting was Sudek's textbook. In the beginning he was inspired by the romantic Czech landscape painting of the mid-1900s. Sudek's early work did not yet have his own personal imprint; rather, it summed up the whole development of Czech photography from the beginning of the twentieth century. There were bromoils and pigments, Art Nouveau-style still lifes, romantic landscapes, and genre pictures. Among these here and there could be found a photograph that was already in Sudek's style: a lonely tree, a lit window, or an early spring landscape.

The influence of impressionism can be seen in his photographs of Kolin Island and the Stromovka. In them, Sudek first became preoccupied with light, which played such an important role in his later work. This light gradually became more spiritual in his first series, "From the Veterans Hospital/Z Invalidovny, 1922–1927," in which he portrayed his veteran friends. For the first time here was a clue to Sudek's personal experience, and it was the last time he freely captured a person in his photographs.

There followed the second important series of photographs, "Saint Vitus," which deals with the completion of the building of the Gothic cathedral in Prague Castle. The whole series consisted of about 100 photographs of which fifteen reached publication in a special 1928 edition of 120 numbered copies. This book was important for Sudek for several reasons: first, it was an official book, published on the ten-year anniversary of the Czechoslovak republic; second, it placed Sudek in the forefront of artistic interest; and last, it confirmed the theme of Prague; a theme he never abandoned and which became the subject of most of his commissioned books. The Saint Vitus series was characteristic of the best of Sudek's oeuvre: monumentality and intimacy, atmosphere and light-filled spirituality of the image, a mingling of the grandeur of the whole with the importance of simple detail.

In the twenties and thirties, between the two world wars, the first generation of Czechoslovak artists was being formed. Full of ideas, vitality, and energy, this generation matured quickly. Artists were opening wide their windows on the world so as to be exposed to current thought and ideas, which they could develop in their own way. Trends changed and knowledge expanded. Photography sped ahead of itself. Influences came from America—the straight photography of unmanipulated negatives; from Germany—the New Objectivity (Neue Sachlichkeit) of Albert Renger Patzsch; the photograms of Man Ray and Christian Schad who basically rejected the copying of reality and created a new realism without the use of the camera—a search for maximum freedom to use fantasy in any combination. In the plastic arts Cubism and Surrealism brought on revolutionary changes, opening new possibilities of free form and loosening the chains of traditional thought. The worldwide crisis of the thirties pointed to social problems. Heard were the last strong echoes of the important influence of Soviet avant-garde

photography and cinematography, which gave proof, just as the Bauhaus did, of the possibility of unusual angles, of different points of view. Composition started to move. We in Czechoslovakia stood in the geographical center of Europe, and these first trends reached us from East and West. Eager and with excited impatience we wanted to make up for a backwardness of many years in our national culture, and we did in a frenetic rush.

Josef Sudek participated in this lively activity. He moved away from the amateur-club movement in 1924 and, together with Funke and others, he founded the Czech Photographic Society. Toward the end of the twenties he cooperated closely with a new publishing house and design center, Druzstevni Prace (Cooperative Work), where the latest thought in contemporary applied art was being practiced. Here he became acquainted with Ladislav Sutnar, photographing the china and glass dinnerware he designed. During this association he made reportage photographs for Druzstevni Prace and its magazine *Panorama*, covering principally workshops, offices, famous writers, and coworkers. But his photographs of Sutnar's designs in particular showed the influences of constructivism and functionalism on him.

In 1928 Sudek proceeded to establish his own photographic business. He photographed children and made portraits of individuals and groups. As an accomplished professional, Sudek never underestimated the value of an honest trade and a job well done. Each order was performed with great care, involving his full energies. Later he made photographic copies of paintings for the superbly printed art monthly *Volne Smery (Free Directions)*, edited by the Cubist painter and intellectual Emil Filla. Sudek and Filla became friends from this association; and because of Filla's exceptional intelligence and erudition their discussions brought

Sudek new insights. Twenty years later Sudek created his own simple Cubist still lifes with glasses and eggs.

In 1933 Druzstevni Prace gave Sudek his first one-man show. In the same year, under the influence of contemporary social trends, Sudek participated in the Social Photography Show ("Filmfoto") held in Prague and arranged by the Left Front. In 1936 he participated in the International Photo Show in Manes. Among the organizers was Emil Filla. Exhibiting with Sudek were Laszlo Moholy-Nagy, Man Ray, John Heartfield, and Alpert. He exhibited there once more in 1938 with six of the foremost avant-garde photographers. This show marked the end of the first part of his photographic life. At this point he had achieved acceptance as a creative photographer, had established a successful commercial studio, and was fully in touch with the Czech intellectual and artistic communities. In photography he had gone from pictorialism via Impressionism to experimental functional compositions. He had found his dominant themes—the city of Prague and the effects of light.

Then came the Second World War. Photographing with large cameras in the streets became suspect under the Nazi occupation. Just as the First World War reached cruelly into Sudek's life, with the loss of his right arm and the subsequent loss of his original bookbinding trade, so now the Second World War brought a change in his work. He locked himself up in his quarters on Ujezd to search out more and more intimate themes among the world of his objects, his surroundings, and his close friends. Externally there remained his garden and the gardens of his artist-friends, the interior of Saint Vitus Cathedral, and the cemetery of Mala Strana with nostalgically abandoned gravestones. It was at this time that Sudek made his greatest

discovery, a discovery that at first glance seemed only technical, yet reached deeply into all his expression and the final realization of each photograph. In 1940, viewing a large contact print made about 1900, he saw that it had a remarkable quality that no enlargement could yield. From this moment Sudek never again made an enlargement. Gradually he returned to some of his negative material from many years past and started to rework it as contact prints. It was a technique that captivated him with its simplicity and its final results.

Sudek always gave priority to tonal value and gradation over grain and contrast. The contact print fulfilled these requirements. A creative refinement led him to the addition of a border frame that surrounded the printed image and became an integral part of the final photograph. Sudek's unusual feeling for perfect craftsmanship, his absolute vision, and his refined execution of technical processes now gave a masterly touch to his almost forty years of work in the form of contact prints of varying sizes—4.5 cm by 6 cm up to 30 cm by 40 cm. For Sudek the choice of paper was decisive. His concentration on technique and the right degree of angle of light and shade was similar to the craft of the draftsman or graphic artist. The number of prints bears witness to his desire for rarity because he made so few from any single negative. He never adhered to a formula; for him, creation was an adventure filled with discovery.

During the Second World War new themes started to appear. "Windows" came about as a result of observing the constantly changing atmosphere in the studio on Ujezd. On his windowsill there were simple objects: bread, glasses, a vase with flowers, a stone, a piece of paper. At first they appeared in the "Windows" photographs accidentally, but gradually they gained importance and became still lifes in themselves.

From 1950 to 1954 he returned to these themes. Around 1968 his simple still lifes developed into structured groupings containing valuable objects such as Art Nouveau-style vases, precious glasses, and carved frames. Many of these were gifts from his friends that had collected on the shelves of this second studio in Uvoz. In the seventies this more rigid form of composition loosened completely and culminated in the "Labyrinths," strangely amorphic compositions created by the life that went on in the studio: trolley tickets thrown about, wrappers from shopping, pieces of aluminum foil, and strings accumulated by time. In all of Sudek's still lifes, more or less arranged, simple or complicated, one discovers not only the object itself, but its life and inner being, an object in which there is always something intriguing and provocative, disquieting and bizarre. To Sudek the objects' life was interwoven with the life of the friends to whom they belonged. That is why some of these still lifes are called "Remembrances" and why they often evoke someone far away or departed.

During the war Sudek also started his photographic theme "Gardens." Through a misty window a strangely twisted tree shined through, photographed in all seasons in differing light. Sometimes the windowpane was not transparent, and the reality of the garden was obscured. Sometimes the garden opened up in poetic delight. To the photographs of his own little garden were added those of the gardens of his artist-friends. The architect Otto Rothmayer was one of these friends. He had taken part in the reconstruction of Prague Castle where Sudek was photographing. His garden was famous, and Sudek after the war photographed its chairs. A new and deep friendship was formed, lasting until Rothmayer's death. This garden became "The Magic Garden." Just as

in the thirties, when Sutnar's inspiring designs and Sudek's photographs formed a unity, so in an entirely different way did Rothmayer's garden with its chairs and objects reflect Sudek's photographs of the fifties. His latent tendency toward the bizarre, his playfulness and provocativeness found here its true expression.

A split between commercial and creative work also came about during the war. Sudek devoted more of his time to his art and less and less to income-producing orders, only to those orders necessary to earn a living.

In the fifties Sudek started to photograph landscapes and the city and its periphery using an unusual format, an antique 10 cm by 30 cm Kodak panorama camera. The collection, entitled *Prague Panoramas*, was published in 1959. His first monograph came out when Sudek was sixty; his last book—*Janacek-Hukvaldy*, about the composer with whom he was so close in spirit—was published when he was seventy-five.

In his lifetime Sudek created an enormous number of photographs; his output was of immense size and importance. His contemporaries were Alfred Stieglitz, Edward Steichen, Edward Weston, Man Ray, Lazlo Moholy-Nagy, John Heartfield, Albert Renger-Patzch, Paul Strand, Dorothea Lange, Andre Kertesz, Jacques-Henri Lartigue, and Ansel Adams—a founding generation of modern photography that was very diverse. Our Sudek was perhaps closest to Weston or Adams, but his work was characterized by a most specific, somehow contemporary, romanticism that was closer to a later generation.

Sudek was an amalgamation of Czech spirit and culture, the influences of which he absorbed during his long and fruitful life. He is marked by the ambience of Prague. He was a good and much beloved person. He was also his own man, a sage,

10

and an eccentric. With Sudek it is possible to admire not only his work but also his life-style, which helped him solve the conflict between creative freedom and personal independence.

I would like to end this introduction the way I completed the catalog to Sudek's last exhibition in Prague, an exhibition that we arranged together for the Museum of Decorative Arts in Prague on the occasion of his eightieth birthday. I quoted Lionel Venturi about Caravaggio, a painter whom Sudek admired so much that he made several still lifes in his honor: "In a time when the whole world was chasing after fame a young man, poor and unknown, humbly started to study a round oblong apple, the shoot of a leaf, a transparent fruit. He felt that there is poetry in everything and he proved that others too wanted to feel it. . . . His light, of course, is not the light of the day or the night, it is altogether not a real light, but rather a stylistic principle, an abstract force and a spiritual quality."

So with Sudek!

ANNA FAROVA
PRAGUE
JANUARY 1978

Translated from Czech by Sonja Bullaty.

11

REMEMBRANCES OF SUDEK

In the old section of Prague, near the river Vltava, an arched doorway leads through a long dark passageway into a courtyard paved with cobblestones; there are a few old chestnut trees and, all around, crumbling apartment houses. Far in back, behind a fence, is a garden overgrown by weeds, and there—in a wooden shack with a crooked little apple tree in front of the window—was Josef Sudek's studio.

To gain entrance one had to have the magic word—or rather, the secret knowledge that behind the vine climbing up the side of the fence there were two exposed wires which, when touched together, rang a bell inside the shack. Primitive, but most efficient. And Sudek could look out from behind the steamed up window and decide whether he wanted the visitor to come in.

Once inside, one's first impression was of incredible clutter, like an antique shop with a feeling of home. There was a small table with three simple chairs, and paintings, sculptures, and art objects everywhere. In the midst of this stood a huge camera on a studio stand, photographic backgrounds that served as room dividers, shelves and closets full of boxes with negatives of all sizes, and phonograph records in every available space. The only clear spot in this seeming chaos was reserved for a homemade record-player, which was always kept open.

Another small room served as office-kitchen-workroom. On one side was an imposing desk piled up from floor to ceiling with more boxes of negatives, papers, and letters, and little notes pinned here and there. On the other side of the room was a table-top hot-plate with a coffee pot, and in front of the window a retouching stand, which most of the time was occupied by Sudkova —as everyone called Sudek's sister—going about her own business. Sudkova was a quiet presence, and I remember her always smiling whether she peeled potatoes or coped with the many visitors. In later years, when Sudek lived in his second studio in Uvoz, she was always concerned about him and would bring him his lunch almost every day.

Then there was the darkroom, truly dark and mysterious, which resembled an alchemist's shop, with all the strange bottles and jars and trays over, under, and inside a long sink. On the other side of the room stood an ancient printer and an enormous 24 by 30 cm enlarger, the creation of Adolf Schneeberger, which had hardly been used since the forties.

I remember the place vividly. I spent many months as Sudek's assistant, helping him mix developers and find negatives, watching him print, and, best of all, sitting together with Sudek and his friends and listening to music. Much later I would come back, together with my husband Angelo Lomeo, to visit again and again and find that things had not really changed.

And so it is especially strange to me that I cannot remember my first meeting with Sudek, nor the first time I entered his world.

The painter Vladimir Fuka, Sudek's assistant during the war years, wrote of this encounter in his memoirs:

After the war, unexpectedly, a new face showed up at Sudek's studio. A Jewish girl. A scarf tied around the pretty, still almost childlike face. She had lost her hair in German concentration camps. She had no one, nobody had returned. The trays in the darkroom that had been deserted were now taken over by Sonja. Photography became her destiny. After a few years the photographer Sonja Bullaty left for the United States.

When I asked Sudek about it later, he said: "You were much too preoccupied with what you had gone through to bother much about any of us or to take in your surroundings." All too true. But I was lucky. I *did* know that I wanted to be a photographer and so somehow the path led me to Sudek.

It was only many years later that the full meaning of those times came to me. Perhaps there was an immediate understanding between us and neither spoke of what was too painful. It was good to face each day at a time, to just be; to see what the weather was like and where we wanted to go to photograph, or when the weather was bad, to work in the darkroom. It was especially good, when there seemed no place to go, that I had a feeling of having found a home in the world of photography.

And so gradually from master and assistant, we became friends. The friendship continued, and grew perhaps even stronger after I left and we corresponded on the back of photographs, exchanged music in the form of packages of phonograph records, and through the laughter and fun we shared on our many visits.

I got to know my native city, Prague, for the first time by climbing the many hills with heavy tripods and cameras. And I remember trying to keep up with Sudek's pace. Somehow the fact that

he had only one arm never seemed a handicap. I was not at all conscious of his disability. He managed so incredibly well with just his left arm. The following paragraph from a letter written shortly after Sudek's death expresses my admiration as well. It was written by Sudek's friend and occasional assistant Dr. Helbich in Prague to Dr. Brumlik, a colleague and friend of Sudek's since the twenties who now lives in New York:

I think of Sudek more and more often of late, not with melancholy, but so that in varying situations I discover how right his life-style was, how peaceable and valid the advice and encouragement he gave me in his kindhearted way and trying not to impose his will. . . . Most often of course I think of him when I photograph landscapes on my long walks. Recently on a wilderness trip I thought especially much about him and I admired him so much in retrospect. On the first day I broke a finger and so had to copy the master even in the respect of onehandedness. How was he able to manage those large machines that he carried around all his life with just one arm? It is really hard to comprehend. And how much he accomplished!

At the time I was there Sudek was still photographing Saint Vitus Cathedral and the Castle— inside and outside—the Royal Gardens, and, when the light was right, the old town, oldest quarter of Prague, and the old cemeteries.

I liked the early evenings when a mysterious sadness crept in and Sudek sat waiting for the last rays of the sun on an old gravestone. It was more familiar here for me, for during the Nazi occupation cemeteries were the only green spaces allowed to those wearing the Jewish star.

Sudek never really was a teacher, he was just

13

himself. It was his single-minded devotion to his work, his joy in life and his vision that stayed with me; the search to say something in his own way, to see life as for the first time. It was his total calm and patience that impressed me more than the actual photographing. And so I just listened to him and only much later understood many of the things he saw.

Besides, I did not at first know much about how a view camera worked, what the different lenses did nor why such a small lens opening and such long exposures were important. So I watched and wondered about the special developers Sudek mixed and the various papers he used for printing. And I was especially fascinated by the way he would suddenly stop and take in a scene with a squint on his face, the left eye almost shut and his hand raised to the right eye to give him a frame for viewing.

Sudek did not often speak about photography, especially since he did not care for theoretical talk. "Theory is all right," he would say, "but it is like eating; when you overeat you get sick." There was not even a way I could see what Sudek was trying to achieve in the photographs. He never printed his pictures right away. Years later he answered one of my letters this way:

That the result of your photos is sometimes different from what you saw you should not mind. You are just reaching the age when that conflict begins. That is why what I photograph I don't print until after at least three months, that way I curse less. The photos which I am sending you for Easter Remembrances were printed two years ago and the one for you is more or less the way it should be, but the others are not so good, well time will tell.

Gradually I began to take in the beauty of the city and to realize that the whole of Sudek's life seemed to revolve around light. I remember one time, in one of the Romanesque halls, deep below the spires of the cathedral—it was as dark as in the catacombs—with just a small window below street level inside the massive medieval walls. We set up the tripod and camera and then sat down on the floor and talked. Suddenly Sudek was up like lightning. A ray of sun had entered the darkness and both of us were waving cloths to raise mountains of ancient dust "to see the light," as Sudek said. Obviously he had known that the sun would reach here perhaps two or three times a year and he was waiting for it.

Nobody knew the city as well as Sudek, whom many called the poet of Prague. Prague is a beautiful old city in the center of Europe, where gothic, baroque, and many styles mingle. It has one of the oldest universities, one of the oldest stone bridges—the beautiful Charles Bridge—and it has an imposing castle in the midst of which Saint Vitus Cathedral grew over the centuries. Josef Sudek was not an educated man, but he was a true man of the people, a folk artist in the best sense, whose genius it was to capture the heart and spirit of this romantic medieval city. Who else would have known and instinctively felt that the way to capture the essence of Saint Vitus and make others comprehend its growth was by photographing the workmen's tools against the background of the Cathedral's majestic architecture? He called the series of photographs "Contrasts." They were published in a limited signed portfolio edition—his first major publication—and they brought him immediate recognition.

Sudek went on to do many books on the city, the Cathedral, and the Charles Bridge. But at the same time there were photographs more intimate and private in character. Little corners of the city, the cemeteries, the gardens, and especially his little garden, as seen over and over again through the window of his studio.

Between the years 1950 and 1959 he finished the enormous book of Prague Panoramas with an 1894 Kodak camera. Here is the recollection of those times by his assistant Jiri Toman.*

I've graduated a good quarter of the Prague Panoramas. It was an incredible sports activity. We'd leave at 9:30 A.M. the latest and be back after sunset. Breakfast in the morning and then only photographing. Three or more cameras, material, a darkroom for the panoramic camera, lenses, tripod, tripod heads, etc. After we'd return everything to Mr. Sudek in the evening I'd get home done in and fall asleep, while Mr. Sudek might go to a concert. Once I too went to a concert. I heard a few bars and then I slept like dead. If Prague Panoramas looks peaceful and quiet, the work which went into it no one can imagine. And then too, few people have seen Prague from all the angles to which Mr. Sudek climbed.

I can say the same for the photographs of the Cathedral, the Castle, and the Royal Gardens. Sudek's vitality was truly incredible. Even in his seventies on many of our visits he would want to show us hard to find places in the city and favorite spots in the gardens overlooking his beloved Prague. And he always managed to go on when we were ready to collapse.

But there were also times of mental rest when Sudek would see friends, listen to music, and sleep late. In 1948 he wrote: "Today is the first of May and I don't know what got into me since I got up easily at 8 o'clock and I started to work right away until 2:00 P.M. That's not happened for a long time." But mostly he was on the go and never tired on the steep hills of Prague.

As incredible as his vitality was Sudek's lack of self-consciousness. He really didn't care what people thought of him or what he looked like. And his curses were notorious.

Dr. Brumlik, who knew him well, told me a story about Sudek that is typical. The Artists Association in Prague, where Dr. Brumlik was secretary at the time, held an exhibition in the thirties. President Masaryk was expected to attend the opening and Sudek wanted to photograph him there. He arrived with his ancient camera, as usual unshaved and in his rumpled old clothes. It did not occur to him to dress differently for this or any other occasion. One of the policemen, always on duty on such occasions, took him for a tramp and refused to admit him. There was an argument at the door. Fortunately, Dr. Brumlik noticed the commotion, and, since he knew the policeman, was able to get Sudek into the exhibition hall.

As the years went by the gnomelike man with the bent shoulders and the sloppy clothing became a familiar figure in the streets of Prague. He would often show up at his friends' exhibitions, though seldom at openings, even of his own shows. He always remained shy and modest, and even as his reputation grew he preferred to remain anonymous.

I remember going to concerts with him. He would choose a seat behind a column, not wanting to be recognized so that he could concentrate better on the music. To the annoyance of people around him he would sometimes tap his foot to the rhythm. He was so absorbed that nothing around him seemed to exist but the intermingling of the voices and themes in the music.

Sudek loved all the arts but music was part of

*Ceskoslovenska Fotografie, 1966 (CS Photography) 1966. Interview with Jiri Toman for Sudek's seventieth birthday.

his life. "You know without music I would be completely lost," he wrote in one of his letters. "Now I'll get started on contemporary music and the very old and primitive folk music." He was forever curious and eager to explore something new in depth.

Some of my fondest memories are of the Tuesday evenings when there was open house at the studio. Work was put aside, friends would gather, and Sudek welcomed all with the words: "There is music . . . and it plays on happily"—his way of saying "life's okay, no matter what," and many of us adopted it as a greeting. Then he would choose a record from his vast collection, and there was no talk while the music was playing. Sudek was far away in his own world. And for me too this was a whole new world as I was introduced to the sound of medieval renaissance and baroque music.

Sudek said that his love for music came from his mother, who sang while she did the laundry when Sudek was a small boy; and that he inherited his gentle disposition from her too. His character, he thought, and his stubborn determination came from his father: "When my father, a painter of interiors, said to himself that he wouldn't work there was no budging him." Of that Sudek too was capable. Certainly there seemed no harshness in him and I often wondered that he was never bitter about his disability or his disappointments.

Sudek was fond of pretty women. I remember one in particular. There was even talk of marriage for a while, but nothing came of it. I suspect that he sometimes played the clown to hide his true feelings; anyway, his great love was photography and his beautiful Prague. Nobody could have withstood the competition for long.

Even in 1974—and Sudek was seventy-eight then—he showed his appreciation for the ladies.

When I sent him photographs of his show at the George Eastman House in Rochester, for which we had lent many prints, I included a few pictures of the museum and museumgoers, and he wrote, "Thanks for the photos and especially for the monumental young lady whom you captured for posterity—I suppose she is meant for me?"

Sudek had a way of shutting out unhappiness. When my friend Bela died in Prague—she had become a good friend of his also—he didn't mention "little mother," as he called her, for over a year. In the same way, in a letter of December 1955, he spoke only in passing of the loss of his own mother because he could not bear to dwell on it. "Right now some publication is going around in my head but about this later. Since I last wrote you the painter Filla died and Vanicek and my mother. Here in the studio not much news except always new things, mostly paintings. At least Sudkova has something to complain about."

And he had a special way of mourning his close friend, the painter Vaclav Sivko. On the back of a print in a letter of July 1974, he wrote: "The figure behind the window in this photograph is Sivko who, I don't know whether I already told you, died of a heart attack, which surprised all of us sadly. After the Mozart record I'll play Scott Joplin. The Mozart is so beautifully sad so perhaps Mr. Joplin will chase the sadness away."

There were professional disappointments as well. Sudek was sometimes criticized for being too formalistic, too static, too romantic, or not socially involved enough. But he would just smile.

I am undoubtedly prejudiced. I love Josef Sudek's photographs and I have always admired them. It is hard to believe today that their sensitive beauty has not always been obvious to others. When I showed impatience that appreciation of his work was slow in coming to this country, he wrote me in 1970:

There is usually a photographic crush to get into shows and I won't try to get in, and if they forget about me nothing will happen but if I should be part of the crowd that doesn't matter either. So let's wait and see. If Mr. X regards me as an antique nothing can be done—that's how he sees me and you won't be able to talk him out of it. You see, to know anything about the present is not so easy. Maybe it'll come to him after he has thoroughly bumped his head into something "modern."

When in the same year it started to look as though a show might finally come about and I proposed the possibility of a book, this was his answer:

With an exhibition and a book of my photographs—hurry slowly—for the following reasons. First it should have a head and a tail and a bit of a spine too, and you must tell me which photographic subjects would have something to say over there and about how many photos there should be. As you know I have the following sizes: 13 by 18, 18 by 24, 24 by 30, 30 by 40, 10 by 30, and everything is now done with borders. And then it has to be decently printed.

And in 1974:

Undoubtedly some of it will fall away but I have a feeling that something will certainly remain. When it's all printed one can undoubtedly pick out a hundred prints as you suggest. Mainly I would not like to include things from my pre-vious books, only perhaps something as a summing up or a beginning of a period. I don't like tea twice brewed. . . . And about who should write it —it would be good if that somebody had some insight into my photo world. That you feel strange, as you write, that though you know me all these years you know little about me that should not bother you, I am pretty confused about me myself and the older I get the more confusing it gets.

"Your theoretical wish to come visit you over there won't happen until in my next life," he wrote in 1970. "Now there's not much time left to have new impressions—not in my visual repertory be-because I can't even realize all that I've bit into here. So rather when you are in Europe again you should slow down your tempo to the speed of a country local and come to Prague for a bit longer."

And in 1972:

Your invitation to the opening of my show in New York just arrived . . . so I'm preparing myself for the hiccups. One is supposed to take a deep breath against it and then have a drink—and so I'll have a drink.

"Hurry slowly" was Sudek's motto throughout his life. It expressed not just patience but a philosophy, the attitude that all's for the best. In rereading his letters it was always reassuring to know that if something could not be achieved or photographed this year he could always come back another time: "This year there was no spring and no early spring either and so what I look forward to all year long went badly and now I have to look forward to next year." This is one of the few times when Sudek spoke of feeling low, as if the fact that spring let him down affected all his thinking. He goes on:

17

*I too get depressed sometimes and I get dis-
gusted with what I am doing and when I feel that
way I think that what I am photographing is probably nonsense but because it won't change anymore and because I have been doing it for so long
maybe it is not bad after all and when I get rid of
the blues then I'll get going again. I have a bit of a
disadvantage because I cannot have a talk with
anyone of my generation since I'm already alone,
but I guess it's better to have a stupid depression
than not to have any problems—that's really bad
when you don't give a damn about anything. It's
a pity we can't occasionally have a good talk in
peace. . . . Often when I play music I think of Mr.
Brumlik and of you.*

And so Sudek's life seems to have been
guided by the weather, which really meant the
light of the seasons. He sometimes photographed
in winter and in fall but most often in spring when
his life seemed to renew itself: "I like to photograph the first hint of spring and all of springtime.
Prague changes and in a person too things
change."
Another time he writes:

*I'm waiting for spring, just like you. . . . Since
Christmas I've had a cold and I can't get rid of it.
Today is Thursday before Easter and so in the
morning I went to take a look around the castle
and into Saint Vitus. The sun was shining happily
but in there it was so cold that after half an hour
I had to hurry home and have tea with a stiff shot
to warm up. I was thinking about the time we
were photographing there; it was warmer then. I
saw something I want to shoot there and when it
gets warmer I'll take another look. . . . I wish you a
nice springtime in good health as in photography.*

Facing page: Self-portrait, "Spring in My Little Garden", 1930's.

18

*On Thursday before Easter, 1970, when it was
actually nice but cold.*

1974 was better weather and he writes:

*Early spring is at my window and so I go a bit
to the gardens to see how spring is awakening. Till
now Saint Peter has conducted everything very
well and so maybe he'll succeed and it won't run
away with itself too fast. . . . Maybe it's just an
attack of spring fever—it will last about two
weeks and after that I'll start to think straight
again.*

And in 1975:

*Because the weather is still more prespring
than spring and it is mostly overcast and the mood
nonphotographic I'll have to bite into my letter
writing. So you see when around Easter the spring
starts to awaken with a bit of sunshine I stroll
around the gardens on Thursday, Good Friday,
Saturday . . . and sometimes in Chotek, Belvedere,
or Strahov or Lobkovic garden I have a conversation with nature, with the trees and the surroundings—sometimes in my mind, sometimes
even aloud. But now I'm wandering off into sim-
plemindedness so I better end this letter.*

Sudek's communication with nature was very
real, almost his religion, and I think of his walk
as a true Easter celebration, a greeting to the new
life around him. A passerby might wonder to
whom he was talking, but not for long. Sudek
would probably draw him into the conversation
and blame the silly talk on "bracha," his crazy
imaginary brother. His sense of the absurd and his
sense of humor were great, and he was the first to

make fun of himself and not permit sentimentality.

When Sudek got older it was almost as if he came out of semihibernation and would gradually reawaken with the approach of spring. In his letters there is the recurrent theme of waiting to capture the elusive rebirth of nature, the eternal renewal. Just so Sudek never seemed to age; he just rested between the various cycles of his creativity. His spirit would come to life again and he came back with new ideas.

But he was not idle in these times, just not taking his heavy equipment outdoors. These were the times when he photographed his window and the many wonderful still lifes, his Easter remembrances, remembrances of friends, his aerial greetings.

Sudek resented the "Nature Morte" still life he was taught in school because to him the things he photographed were never dead. The objects he chose for his arrangements were part of his experience and his life, often the ingredients of his frugal meal—a piece of bread, an egg, an onion, or an apple. And he surrounded these simple things with a magic light so that we feel how important they were to him. Through his eyes we see them in a new way. I will never forget the chaos on his table from which he created the incredible photographs called "Labyrinths." The crumpled papers that look like a surrealistic construction were the accumulated wrappers of sandwiches—and other odds and ends—which his sister Sudkova would bring him every day for his lunch.

Perhaps too those still lifes touch us so because there seems to be a private life within them that the turmoil outside cannot touch. A long time ago the editor Jan Rezac spoke of the two friends and pioneers of Czechoslovak photography, Sudek

and Funke; and, he called Funke the experimenter and Sudek the harmonizer.

Sudek lived through difficult times—two world wars and years of political upheavals and dissent. Sometimes he was accused of being aloof or apart from the mainstream of events, but I believe that through the simple reassurance in the meaning of everyday objects he was able to point the way to reality, to sanity and to continuity, and it was this harmony and peacefulness that brought so many people of such differing backgrounds to him. Almost as if coming to an oasis to rest and to take nourishment before facing a crazy world again.

In 1960 there was a show in Prague entitled "Sudek in the Graphic Arts," a tribute to the man and the environment he had created. Twenty-two artists participated with paintings, drawings, etchings, photographs, lithographs, sculptures; several generations of friends and people in the arts whose life was influenced by his work and more often by his life-style and his philosophy. Many were the same artists who gathered at Sudek's place for the Tuesday evenings of music. They would come back at other times alone to bring Sudek their work to look at, sometimes to bring them as gifts. "That's not too bad, you know, there's something there, you're getting it," and it was enough encouragement for his friend to go home and get back to work. Or people came with problems and Sudek would listen patiently. Sometimes, when he sensed that the problem was financial, he would just slip a few crowns in their pocket to help out.

For Sudek understood poverty. When he was young he had to struggle to gain financial independence but as soon as his photography business became successful the material side was of little interest to him. In later years income came from

Facing Page: Portrait of Sudek on his eightieth birthday, March 17, 1976, by Sonja Bullaty.

21

the many books he produced. Sudek certainly was not poor although he lived almost like a pauper, some thought even like a miser. He liked the simplest food, especially with a tall glass of beer, he did not care for clothes, rent was cheap, and so his only luxury was the record collection and even that grew mostly by gifts from his friends. The value of money just was of no concern to Sudek.

Though people came for advice he did not often give it other than "take a stiff shot with a pickle and go to sleep for your hangover." He was a kind of conscience to all of us. He made us rethink our values, and he made us laugh when we were depressed. His great sense of humor made many get back on the right road.

The works of art, the record collection, and the gifts and fragments accumulated as did the negatives and prints, and finally Sudek left the old place and moved to new surroundings and it was not long before the new studio began to look just as crowded as the old one. The new place was on a steep hill going to the castle and it overlooked the gardens. I remember knocking on the window after some years' absence—we had come to Prague to visit him on his eightieth birthday—and there he was, obviously pleased and with a smile of welcome. He did not even seem surprised, as if he'd been expecting us all along. We continued a conversation started long ago and reminisced and laughed and joked and drank toasts and then went to visit friends and had a very private celebration in Sudek's favorite pub. The pub was full of smoke and the smell of beer, and somehow all the years between were gone, and Sudek was always the same: a constant, a landmark full of life and joy, which we all thought would go on forever.

In the months that I worked with Sudek as his assistant and "apprentice-martyr," as he called me, I got used to the requests from people who wanted me to find negatives of their wedding; the prints were not yet made when the first child arrived. I wish I could have found the "photographic note" that Sudek took of me while I photographed him and my friend Bela at the Castle Krivoklat. It is somewhere with thousands of unprinted negatives, now part of a museum archive. I wish too that I had the portraits that he took of friends, and some of me just before I left for the United States. He had promised to send them, and somehow there always seemed time.

When we visited Sudek the last time, the weather was gray and drizzly—somehow typical Sudek light—and so I made a few photographs of him. Since I did not remember seeing any of his photographs of this beautiful street where he now lived I asked him about it. "Someday I'll get around to it," and we both laughed, and so I made a last frame of the street just for him, and the street is empty. Somehow I can still see him there, in the streets of Prague.

I think of Sudek often but no longer with sadness. The other day I saw a flock of wild geese overhead. They were flying straight and free toward a far-off destination, and I thought how Sudek's life followed a clear path to a goal no one or nothing could distract him from. And how his great love for music, especially medieval music, applied to his art as well. Certain themes recur— the window, the streets and courtyards of Prague, the Bohemian countryside, the small gardens, remembrances. This may be what gives Sudek's photographs their special dimension—the joy of exploring the same theme again and again and always coming up with new variations.

There is the crooked little apple tree in front of his window; the everchanging windowpane with Cubist or Impressionist patterns; the still

22

lifes created from the clutter on his unbelievable desk. These are not whimsies; they were a search for meaning in the everyday objects around us, and from those simple things he created his own harmony, the harmony he so much admired in music.

Sudek was not afraid of lyricism, of showing his emotion in his work. He always remained himself. Through Sudek's window we look out at his world, and we are allowed to look into a very private land of dreams.

. . . and always there is music . . .

JOSEF SUDEK – A SELF-PORTRAIT

Here are Sudek's own words from various interviews and letters. He had a most wonderful and original way of expressing his thoughts; as in everything else, he was an individualist. To translate him was somewhat of a problem, and I fear it was not always possible to convey the full gusto of his remarks. Still, what comes through is his complete sincerity and the sense of humor he directed at himself and at the world. Sudek disliked big words and often laughed when they were applied to his photographs. He was very much a man of the people—from his humble childhood to his deliberate later life-style—but his taste in art and music was most sophisticated and refined.

I grew up in Kutna Hora. When as a boy I saw the Gothic art I looked like a rabbit at newly fallen snow. I was not very educated; growing up with the Gothic all around me and I did not even know it.

I did not have good grades in school and everybody predicted I'd wind up on the gallows or if I was lucky I'd become a shepherd. This did not much upset me, after all what's nicer than to have a job in the open air.

When you are fourteen and they ask you what you would like to be you think to yourself—why don't they just leave me alone.

Photography, that was an adventure. . . . Take an enlarger for instance; that was a funny box, where you put a negative on top, paper on the bottom and then you took the whole thing someplace in an open space without buildings, put it down on the ground, and exposed for several minutes by daylight. When I wanted to enlarge, that was not so simple, I had to wait for the weather not to be changeable, so the exposure would be even. That was not photography, that was meteorology. Today it is easier, only today I don't enlarge anymore. But then someday you have to decide.

I used to like to read, but books then were expensive. That's why I decided to become a bookbinder. The reason was obvious. I thought that I could at least read all the books for free.

When the war came, the First World War, I had to go to the front in Italy. The landscape was beautiful—as long as there was no shooting.

The war destroyed my arm, later I lost it. Of course I did not enjoy that, but I was consoling myself that at least I did not lose my head. That would have been worse.

Every young person wants to be something. I had to face this again after the war. A tobacconist shop, that did not feel right. Somebody got me a job in an office. I thought about it a lot and finally I went there and told them: I don't want the job—because it was springtime and the sparrows were chirping.

To earn a living I continued to try photographing. Then when I entered the School of Graphic Arts, that was a new world. Professor Karel Novak was a noble gentleman, intelligent, you could tell right away, because he withstood my cursing and statements the way they stayed in my vocabulary from the war. I also liked that he would show a collection of photos and would say nothing. Isn't that beautiful when one doesn't say anything to the photographs.

Professor Novak . . . belonged to the old school. For example, we photographed still lifes arranged in the fashion of the so-called "modern" style . . . it was so artificial. I returned to still lifes later on . . . but in quite a different way.

When a person wants to accomplish something he must go and listen to someone wiser. I went to the painter Filla. He understood painting and art in general, so once I admitted to him that at first I used to like patriotic Kitsch and only later did I come to Picasso. Filla smiled and said, it would have been worse the other way around.

When I was young I was a fool. I thought too much. Fortunately I did not say it out loud. If I had, the echo would horrify me to this day.

Sometimes youth takes on too much, but that probably doesn't matter. At least then in older age there is something to finish up.

Friendships with people, things, and landscapes; they have made their mark upon me in some sort of way. One of my oldest friends was Jaromir Funke, then a young photographer of my own age. . . . We were both members of a group of amateur photographers, and at the time—the beginning of the twenties—we were considered quite progressive. But . . . we were also particular, very demanding, and we tolerated no compromise. For this reason we were banned from the Photo Club; we were too aggressive and critical.

I often went with Funke after something that we decided on in our heads and no way, nothing came of it. And at the same time, all of a sudden, we did something else—and that was it. Discovery— that's important. First comes the discovery. Then follows the work. And then sometimes something from it remains.

Together with some other photographers, we founded the Czech Photographic Society in 1924 ... We set up in opposition to our father's generation and protested against the artistic tendencies in photography. We dedicated ourselves to photography as a documentary medium, we advocated the integrity of the negative and energetically opposed all manipulation and complicated techniques that came under the heading of "artistic processes," such as bromoil, carbon, gum, etc., and we also rejected retouching and aftertreatment of the negative.

One of my first pictures was a sprinkler wagon pulled by horses. I threw the negative away—one should not do that. Many times I was sorry that I did not have it. Horses pulling a sprinkler wagon! That would be quite a rarity today.

My friend Funke was an intellectual . . ., he represented the avant-garde Czech photographers . . . but we were both romantics at heart, otherwise we would never have been able to work the way we did. Funke died in 1945.

One cannot escape being influenced by others, but these influences were only good to the extent that they forced me to go my own way. I met the Czech-American Ruzicka early in my life and through him the photography of [Clarence H.] White. At the time I did not yet know that all mystery lies in the shadow areas. When Dr. Ruzicka arrived from the U.S.A. he told me often: expose for the shadows, the rest will come by itself —he was right. . . . But how to master the technique, that I did not know yet.

The painter Frinta . . . recommended me to the publisher Druzstevni Prace, whom I later supplied with photographs for his magazine Panorama. Toward the end of the twenties and during the thirties I also made portraits and documentary pictures for this publisher, as well as advertising photos of glass and porcelain objects designed by the well-known Czech designer Ladislav Sutnar. . . . Frinta knew the photographs of the [Saint Vitus] Cathedral, which I had taken for my own pleasure from 1924 on. . . . He suggested making an edition of 120 signed copies, a bibliophile album with 15 photographs.

My collaboration with Druzstevni Prace . . . was very important to me. The publishers . . . were really a combine that provided its members not only with an excellent choice of high-quality books, but also with articles. . . . It was all very exciting.

I worked with a group of friends, we had many similar ideas, and it would have been difficult to have found another circle in which I could have worked with such enthusiasm for so many years. My work with Druzstevni brought me not only material gain but also intellectual recognition.

One learns everywhere. I made advertising photos too, shoes for instance; it was interesting work for its detail, its accuracy. I also photographed underwear—women's was fun, men's less so.

As soon as I had earned enough money to pay for my rent and food, I closed the studio and worked for myself. You should never lose contact with that which is close to your heart; at the most you can make an interruption for half a year. If it is longer you lose the thread and never find it again.

In 1933 I took part in the Exhibition of Social Photography, as well as holding my first one-man

25

show in Prague. I continued photographing Prague, above all the Castle, about which I published two books after the war, as well as a book on the city itself.

I came across a photographic reproduction from around 1900 that fascinated me through its texture and excellent quality. It was 30 by 40 cm and showed a statue in Chartres. On closer inspection I established that it was a contact print. From that day on—it was 1940—I never made another enlargement.

I print my photographs exactly the way a graphic artist prints the engraving or the etching on his printing press. I want nothing else but that the camera with its lens delivers what I myself put in front of it.

I make all exposures by guessing so I can't guarantee their accuracy (when giving technical information for a magazine article), except that I use the smallest lens opening.

When I began to photograph my window during the war I discovered that very often something was going on under the window that became more and more important to me. An object of some kind, a bunch of flowers, a stone, in short, something separated this still life and made an independent picture. I believe that photography loves banal objects, and I love the life of objects. I am sure you know the fairy tales of Andersen: when the children go to bed, the objects come to life, toys, for example. I like to tell stories about the life of inanimate objects, to relate something mysterious: the seventh side of a dice.

It would have bored me extremely to have restricted myself to one specific direction for my whole life, for example, landscape photography. A photographer should never impose such restrictions upon himself.

I was deeply attached to the architect Otto Rothmayer. . . . I met him in Prague Castle where I was making pictures for myself and for various architects. One of them told me about the beauty of Rothmayer's garden. I am very fond of town gardens, and I particularly wanted to get to know this garden. When Rothmayer asked me to photograph his chairs, I immediately accepted, but it was really his garden I wanted to photograph. Rothmayer was pleased with the photographs and we became friends. . . . We were friends right up until his death.

Rothmayer was an artist who—like myself—had no great regard for the rationally definable.

The greater part of the panorama pictures were made after Rothmayer's death, and only a few were taken in his garden.

I photographed first and foremost the city of Prague, and the book Prague Panoramas with 288 photographs appeared in 1959. It was photographed with a Kodak 1894, which I found in a small town in Morava during World War II. It has only two shutter speeds and makes negatives of 10 by 30 cm.

Meanwhile I'm trying to photograph with a 30 by 40 camera and it is worth shit and a big one. So maybe I'm on the right track of learning it. It just looks all different in there than on the smaller format I'm used to, and for the time being I don't know or rather I don't see how to go about it. The technical mastering of it is very hard, everything *takes too long and I'm so clumsy, so unpractical, in a word stupid.*

I don't have many people in my photographs, especially in the landscapes. To explain this, you see, it takes me a while before I prepare everything. Sometimes there are people there, but before I'm ready they go away, so what can I do, I won't chase them back.

I was inspired to make "Remembrances" by gifts from my friends and I tried to honor the givers . . . by these compositions.

I have no particular leaning toward . . . the all-too-clearly defined; I prefer the living, the vital, and life is very different from geometry; simplified security has no place in life.

Everything around us, dead or alive, in the eyes of a crazy photographer mysteriously takes on many variations, so that a seemingly dead object comes to life through light or by its surrounding. And if the photographer has a bit of sense in his head maybe he is able to capture some of this—and I suppose that's lyricism.

When a person likes his profession and tries hard to overcome the difficulties that are connected with it, then he is glad if at least something of what he tried to do succeeds. I think that is enough for a lifetime. And while you're at it you work up a real sweat and that's a bonus.

I used to be fascinated by painting; now music has taken the place of painting.

One day I just couldn't resist it. When the musicians of the Czech Philharmonic told me: "Josef,

come with us, we are going to Italy to play music," I told myself, fool that you are, you were there, and you did not enjoy that beautiful country when you served as a soldier for the emperor's army. And so I went with them on this unusual excursion. In Milan we had a lot of applause and acclaim and we traveled down the Italian boot until one day we came to that place—I had to disappear in the middle of the concert; in the dark I got lost but I had to search. Far outside the city toward dawn, in the fields bathed by the morning dew, I finally found the place. But my arm wasn't there—only the poor peasant farmhouse was still standing in its place. They had brought me into it that day when I was shot in the right arm. They could never put it together again, and for years I was going from hospital to hospital, and I had to give up my bookbinding trade. The Philharmonic people apparently even made the police look for me, but I somehow could not get myself to return from this country. I turned up in Prague some two months later. They didn't reproach me, but from that time on I never went anywhere anymore and I never will.

What would I be looking for when I didn't find what I wanted to find? At most I travel to Moravia to the region of Leos Janacek, his Hukvaldy—but here I am again, talking about music. In music you find everything. . . . Music has to be inside you.

I have a feeling that (my love for music) started with my mother's singing. She always sang when she did the laundry. And in school as a boy I also sang. But I was so lazy that I only liked the singing and not the notes. And so to this day I don't know how to read music. When I came to Prague for the first time in 1910, the first thing I wanted to do was to go to the National Theater, to hear what an

27

opera actually was all about. I had only heard about it; that it was a big building, that they sang there, and that there is music. . . . After the war I went for symphonic music. I was not much wiser after the first concerts, but then it all fell into place. I know that opera never forgave me that I abandoned her. I went for symphonies and concertos. Much later only did I discover solo instruments and quartets.

I heard the first phonograph when I was a boy. In Nove Dvory there was a castle and the director had a Gramophone with a horn; they used to have it in the window and they listened in the garden. We listened on the other side of the fence. I bought my first phonograph in 1928.

Music influences my work but how, I could not tell you. Either you feel it or you think you do and it is not so. But in any case it gives you a push. Music always led me to something. If you take photography seriously you must also get interested in another art form. For me it is music. This listening to music shows up in my work like a reflection in a mirror. I relax and the world looks less unpleasant, and I can see that all around there is beauty, such as the music.

Janacek-Hukvaldy . . . appeared in 1971, but the pictures are much older. They come from the time when I was in love with the music of Leos Janacek, and I created it from a feeling of friendship.

I told myself that if Janacek has such beautiful music, he had to have a beautiful landscape too—where the music came from and that I should go there and take a look. I wanted to but for a long time nothing. Until the publisher Klika urged me to take the trip. Those were wonderful experi-

ences: the landscape, the ruin of the castle, and the trees and hillsides. A year later I went again. I told myself that I'll photograph it. But again, as always, it took a while. At first I went there every year, then I would skip one; the material accumulated but still no book. . . . What was finally published, the book Janacek-Hukvaldy is a result of a great effort about something.

I will probably not be able to think through or to finish any more projects. It is as if I were to say that it would be a nice excursion on foot to Hukvaldy and back. But I could not make it all the way anymore and certainly not back. That is already like a fairy tale, but also a risk and an uncertainty. Years of searching, but at a certain moment there does not remain enough time.

I never cease to be surprised at young people's interest in my pictures. I can only explain it in the context of a certain longing for romanticism, for good old craftsmanship. But that will pass, and in a few years their interest will lie somewhere different. But prophesies are always risky. The critics of my generation never visualized photography as an independent branch of art; today this is accepted as a matter of course.

I don't like the discussions about whether photography is an art. Even though I think that if it would be just a craft I would not have stayed with it all my life.

Every young person has talent. But talent alone is not enough. I once knew a painter with talent. He drank and he drank. And it ended up as if he had no talent at all.

This profession does not have a long tradition. A hundred years? What is that? A lot depends on skill. Until now it is not possible to photograph with the eyes only. When I want to accomplish something I do it all alone. That's why I don't go into color photography, that is a complicated profession that I don't know. To have one's material developed elsewhere, that would bother me.

When a photographer decides on a theme, he wants to finish, put it all together, and close a chapter. But that's forcing it. It is better rather to do other things too and to live. When something doesn't come together by itself it cannot be forced. The photos then look tired.

One should do what one knows. I was putting together photographs for something called an exhibition. For Prague and Brno. I thought about a comprehensive retrospective. But is that possible? Can a person fit? I just about managed to put the photographs into "Remembrances," "Labyrinths," and "Walks."

I believe a lot in instinct. One should never dull it by wanting to know everything.

One shouldn't ask too many questions but do what one does properly, never rush, and never torment oneself.

SOURCES

1. *Mlady Svet (Young World)*, March 1976, Prague. Interview with Rudolf Krestan.
2. *Kvety (Flowers)*, September 14, 1968, Prague.
3. *Camera*, April 1976, Switzerland. Interview with Anna Farova.
4. *Ceskoslovenska Fotografie (CS Photography)*, 1966. Interview with Milon Novotny for Sudek's seventieth birthday.
5. *Memoirs by* Vladimir Fuka.
6. Letters to Sonja Bullaty, March 22, 1950, and September 23, 1949.
7. *Literarni Mesicnik (Literary Monthly)*, April 1974, Czechoslovakia. Interview with Miroslav Khol.
8. Interview about music with Marie Kulijevycova, Prague. Date and publication not verified.

PREFACE TO THE PLATES

It is many years now since I first suggested to Sudek that a book of his photographs be published in this country. The problem was that in his lifetime he made so many photographs that he could not face up to choosing. But gradually over the years he made up little portfolios of the various periods of his work and sent them or he gave them to us on our many visits.

The last time we visited—for his eightieth birthday—I brought him a letter saying that the monograph I had written to him about was going to be published soon, and we were able to discuss it in person. Sudek had just finished putting together two different shows—for Prague and for Brno— to be shown later that year. Out of a box, one by one, he showed us the photographs for the retrospective to be held at the Museum of Decorative Arts in Prague, which Anna Farova had helped him organize. I realized that the photographs he had been giving to us were a close parallel—that he had wanted us to have a rounded statement of his life's work.

It was not easy to choose from the many beautiful photographs of such a devoted and productive life but it is my hope that Sudek would have approved of this book. I wish I could hear his comments.

THE PLATES

2

21

22

23

54

61

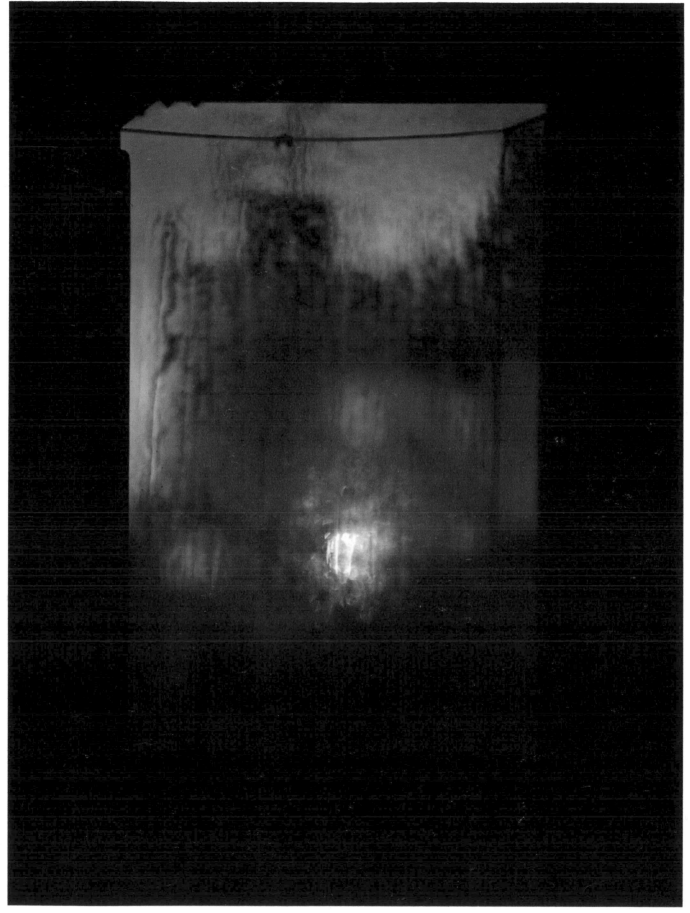

74

NOTES TO THE PLATES

All images reproduced in this book are made from original contact prints except where indicated.
*Reproduced from original enlargement.

Frontispiece p. 1 EASTER REMEMBRANCES, 1969, reproduced same size

Frontispiece p. 2 LABYRINTH IN MY ATELIER, 1960, negative size 24 x 30 cm

page 19 SELF-PORTRAIT, SPRING IN MY LITTLE GARDEN, 1930's, reproduced same size

1* MORNING TROLLEY (Prague), 1924, negative size 9 x 12 cm

2* SUNDAY AFTERNOON ON KOLIN ISLAND, 1924–1926, negative size 9 x 9 cm, reproduced same size

3* SUNDAY AFTERNOON ON KOLIN ISLAND, 1926, negative size 9 x 9 cm

4* SUNDAY AFTERNOON ON KOLIN ISLAND, 1924–1926, negative size 9 x 9 cm

5* Z INVALIDOVNY (From the Veterans Hospital), 1922–1927, negative size 9 x 12 cm

6* IN CHURCH, 1925, negative size 9 x 9 cm

7* MORNING VIADUCTS (Prague), 1926, negative size 9 x 9 cm

8* CONTRASTS, SAINT VITUS CATHEDRAL, 1924–1925, negative size 9 x 9 cm

9 CONTRASTS, SAINT VITUS CATHEDRAL, 1925–1928, negative size 13 x 18 cm, reproduced same size

10 CONTRASTS, SAINT VITUS CATHEDRAL, 1925–1928, negative size 13 x 18 cm, reproduced same size

11 MILENA, 1942, bromoil print dated 1945, negative size 13 x 18 cm, reproduced same size

12 NUDE, 1951–1954, negative size 18 x 24 cm, reproduced same size

13 PORTRAIT OF MY FRIEND FUNKE, 1924, negative size 24 x 30 cm

14 PORTRAIT OF THE PAINTER VACLAV SIVKO, 1955, negative size 13 x 18 cm, reproduced same size

15 WINTER FROM THE WINDOW OF MY ATELIER, 1940–1954, negative size 18 x 24 cm

16 SUMMER FROM THE WINDOW OF MY ATELIER, 1940–1954, negative size 18 x 24 cm

17 FROM THE WINDOW OF MY ATELIER, 1940–1954, negative size 13 x 18 cm, reproduced same size

18* FROM THE WINDOW OF MY ATELIER, 1940–1945, negative size 13 x 18 cm, reproduced same size

19 FROM THE WINDOW OF MY ATELIER, 1940–1954, negative size 24 x 30 cm

20 EVENING ON CHARLES BRIDGE (Prague), 1940–1950, negative size 13 x 18 cm, reproduced same size

21* A WALK ON KAMPA ISLAND, 1947, negative size 13 x 18 cm, reproduced same size

22 Photographic note, negative size 6 x 9 cm, reproduced same size

23 SPRING IN STRAHOV GARDEN, from the series "The Coming of Spring to Prague," 1963, negative size 22 x 27 cm

24 SPRING LABYRINTH ON CHARLES BRIDGE, from the series "The Coming of Spring to Prague," 1959–1969, negatixe size 24 x 30 cm

25 A WALK IN THE MAGIC GARDEN, panorama, 1954, negative size 10 x 29.2 cm, reproduced same size

26 PRAGUE PANORAMA, panorama, 1950–1956, negative size 10 x 29.2 cm, reproduced same size

27 FROM THE BOHEMIAN COUNTRYSIDE, Photographic Note, negative size 6 x 9 cm, reproduced same size

28 A WALK IN THE ROYAL GARDENS, 1946, negative size 11.6 x 16, reproduced same size

29 A WALK IN THE CEMETERY OF MALA STRANA, 1940–1946, negative size 16 x 22 cm, reproduced same size

30 A WALK IN THE CEMETERY OF MALA STRANA, 1946, negative size 16 x 22 cm, reproduced same size

31 A WALK IN THE CEMETERY OF MALA
    STRANA, 1946, negative size 13 x 18 cm,
    reproduced same size

32 No title, 1950–1964, negative size 11.6 x 16 cm,
    reproduced same size

33 BREAD AND EGG, bromoil print, 1951, negative
    size 13 x 18 cm, reproduced same size

34 ONIONS, 1950–1954, negative size 9 x 12 cm,
    reproduced same size

35 GLASSES AND EGGS, 1952, negative size
    18 x 24 cm

36 A JOKE, 1953, negative size 9 x 12 cm,
    reproduced same size

37 LOVERS, from the series "Remembrances,"
    1960, negative size 30 x 40 cm

38 A SUMMER SHOWER IN THE MAGIC
    GARDEN, 1954–1959, negative size 18 x 24 cm

39 From the series "Remembrances," 1954–1959,
    negative size 18 x 24 cm, reproduced same size

40 A WALK IN THE MAGIC GARDEN, 1954–1959,
    negative size 24 x 30 cm

41 REMEMBRANCE OF MR. MAGICIAN, the
    garden of architect Rothmayer, 1959, negative
    size 30 x 40 cm

42 LABYRINTHS, 1969, negative size 24 x 30 cm

43 THE WINDOW OF MY ATELIER, 1969, negative
    size 18 x 24 cm, reproduced same size

44 LABYRINTH ON MY TABLE, 1967, negative
    size 24 x 30 cm

45 EASTER REMEMBRANCES, 1968–1970, negative
    size 11.6 x 16 cm, reproduced same size

46 From the series "Remembrances," 1968–1970,
    negative size 24 x 30 cm

47 STILL LIFE, 1936, negative size 13 x 18 cm

48 No title, negative size 13 x 18 cm, reproduced
    same size

49 PRAGUE AT NIGHT, 1958, negative
    size 24 x 30 cm

50 PRAGUE AT NIGHT, Photographic Note, 1958,
    negative size 6 x 9 cm, reproduced same size

51 PRAGUE AT NIGHT, Photographic Note, 1958,
    negative size 6 x 9 cm, reproduced same size

52 A WALK ON KAMPA ISLAND, bromoil print,
    1950, negative size 13 x 18 cm, reproduced
    same size

53 Photographic Note, 1955–1970, negative size
    6 x 9 cm, reproduced same size

54 From the series "Vanished Statues in Mionsi,"
    1969, negative size 11.6 x 16 cm, reproduced
    same size

55 From the series "Vanished Statues in Mionsi,"
    1955–1970, negative size 13 x 18 cm,
    reproduced same size

56 From the series "Vanished Statues in Mionsi,"
    1965, negative size 18 x 24 cm

57 From the series "Vanished Statues in Mionsi,"
    1955–1970, negative size 11.6 x 16 cm,
    reproduced same size

58 A WALK IN THE GARDEN OF THE LADY
    SCULPTOR, 1957, negative size 6 x 15.3 cm,
    reproduced same size

59 THE COMING OF AUTUMN, 1932, negative
    size 13 x 18 cm, reproduced same size

60 No title, 1967, negative size 18 x 24 cm

61* A WALK ON TROJA ISLAND, 1940–1945,
    negative size 13 x 18 cm, reproduced same size

62 THE COMING OF SPRING, 1968, negative
    size 24 x 30 cm

63 FROM THE BESKYD MOUNTAINS, panorama,
    1950–1956, negative size 10 x 29.2 cm,
    reproduced same size

64 LANDSCAPE IN STREDOHORI, panorama,
    1954, negative size 10 x 29.2 cm, reproduced
    same size

65 TWO WET LEAVES, 1932, negative size
    13 x 18 cm, reproduced same size

66 REMEMBRANCES OF E. A. POE, 1959, negative
    size 30 x 40 cm

67 From the series "Remembrances," 1950, negative
    size 18 x 24 cm, reproduced same size

68 A WALK IN THE GARDEN OF THE LADY
    SCULPTOR, 1957, negative size 24 x 30 cm

69 From the series "Remembrances," 1953, negative
    size 13 x 18 cm, reproduced same size

70 THE FORGOTTEN STAIRCASE, from the series
    "Remembrances," 1950, negative size 13 x 18 cm,
    reproduced same size

71 UNEASY NIGHT, from the series
    "Remembrances," 1959, negative size 13 x 18 cm,
    reproduced same size

72 From the series "Remembrances," 1959, negative
    size 18 x 24 cm, reproduced same size

73 REMEMBRANCES OF SONJA AND ANGELO
    (second variation), 1968–1969, negative size
    24 x 30 cm

74 AERIAL REMEMBRANCES, for Dr. Brumlik,
    1971, negative size 20 x 25 cm

75 AT THE JANACEKS, from *Janacek-Hukvaldy*,
    1948, negative size 11.6 x 16 cm, reproduced
    same size

76 A WHITE ROSE, 1954, negative size 18 x 24 cm

JOSEF SUDEK: A BRIEF BIOGRAPHY

1896 • Josef Sudek is born on March 17 in the town of Kolin on the River Labe (Elbe) in Bohemia. His father, a house painter, dies when Sudek is three years old.

1911–13 • Sudek is apprenticed to a bookbinder. A fellow worker introduces him to amateur photography.

1915 • He is inducted into the army.

1916 • He is posted at the Italian front. After eleven months, he is seriously injured.

1917 • Sudek suffers the loss of his right arm. He spends the next three years in hospitals and decides to become a photographer.

1920 • Sudek joins the Club for Amateur Photographers in Prague.

1922 • He studies photography with Professor Karel Novak at the School of Graphic Art in Prague for two years.

1922–27 • Sudek makes a series of photographs of disabled soldiers at the Veterans Hospital, called "Z Invalidovny."

1924 • Josef Sudek, Jaromir Funke, and a group of other avant-garde photographers found the Czech Photographic Society.

1924–28 • Sudek photographs the reconstruction of Saint Vitus Cathedral. He contrasts the tools of the workmen with the grandeur of the architecture and calls the series "Contrasts." The series is published in 1928 by Druzstevni Prace in a limited edition of 120 copies, with 15 signed original prints. This earns him the title of Official Photographer of the City of Prague.

1926 • After a brief stop to attend the Congress of War Veterans in Belgium, Sudek goes on a two month trip to Italy. This is the last time he will leave Czechoslovakia.

1928–36 • He continues his association with the publishing house Druzstevni Prace, and becomes co-editor and illustrator of the magazine *Panorama* and, later, *Zijeme*. In his studio he does advertising, commercial, and portrait photography, and continues to make landscapes and views of Prague.

1933 • Sudek's first one-man show. He also participates in a group show "Social Photography." His first calendar and edition of postcards are published.

1936 • Sudek participates in the International Photography Exhibition in Prague, together with Laszlo Moholy-Nagy, John Heartfield, Man Ray, Alexandr Rodcenko, Alpert, and others.

1938 • Sudek and Funke exhibit with other avant-garde Czech photographers in Prague.

1939 • Sudek participates in the last prewar exhibit in Prague, "100 Years of Photography."

1940 • Sudek sees a contact print, 30 x 40 cm, of a statue in Chartres Cathedral, which impresses him so much that from then on he decides to use mostly large-format cameras and make only contact prints. He continues to photograph Prague, the Cathedral, Charles Bridge, and the Bohemian countryside.

1940–45 • He starts the series "Windows" in his studio and continues with his still lifes. Meets architect Otto Rothmayer.

1945–60 • Sudek photographs the garden of Otto Rothmayer in a series called "The Magic Garden" and does another series called "The Garden of the Lady Sculptor." He continues to photograph panoramas of Prague and the countryside, and publishes several books.

1960 • A major show in Prague, "Sudek in the Arts," brings together the works of twenty-two artists—paintings, drawings, sculpture, etchings, lithographs, photographs—that portray Sudek and his surroundings. The artists pay tribute to the man they love and admire and who has influenced their own work.

1961 • Sudek is the first photographer to receive the title "Artist of Merit" from the Czechoslovak government.

1966 • He is awarded the "Order of Work" in Czechoslovakia. One-man shows of certain periods of his work are held in Prague and Brno.

1971 • On March 17, Sudek's seventy-fifth birthday, a one-man show is held at the studio of Sonja Bullaty and Angelo Lomeo in New York.

1972 • The Neikrug Gallery in New York celebrates the opening of a Sudek exhibition on March 17.

1973 • The Light Gallery in New York holds a Sudek show in March.

1974 • A Sudek retrospective is held at the International Museum of Photography, George Eastman House, Rochester, New York.

1976 • There are two different retrospective shows of Sudek's work in Czechoslovakia, one in Prague, another in Brno. Sudek dies on September 15, 1976.

1977 • A retrospective Sudek show is held at the International Center of Photography in New York. Exhibits are also held in Germany, England, Scotland, France, and Italy.

BOOKS AND PORTFOLIOS

1928 • SVATY VIT (Saint Vitus) by Josef Sudek. Fifteen original prints, published in a signed limited edition of 120 copies by Druzstevni Prace, Czechoslovakia.

1947 • PRAZSKY HRAD (Prague Castle). Photographs by Josef Sudek, text by Rudolf Roucek. SFINX Bohumil Janda Praha, Czechoslovakia.

1947 • BAROQUE PRAGUE. Photographs by Josef Sudek, text in English by Arne Novak. Ceska Graficka Unie (Czech Graphic Union), Czechoslovakia.

1947 • MAGIC IN STONE. Photographs by Josef Sudek. Lincolns-Prager Ltd. Publishers, London.

1948 • PRAHA—JOSEF SUDEK. Text by Vitezslav Nezval. In Czech, Russian, English, and French. Svoboda, Prague.

1948 • NAS HRAD (Our Castle). Photographs by Josef Sudek, text by A. Wenig, J. R. Vilimek, Prague.

1956 • JOSEF SUDEK FOTOGRAFIE. Introduction by Lubomir Linhart. SNKLHU (State Publishing House of Literature, Music, and Art), Prague.

1958 • LAPIDARIUM NARODNIHO MUZEA (Lapidarium of the National Museum), Prague.

1959 • PRAHA PANORAMATICKA (Prague Panoramas). Photographs by Josef Sudek, poem by Jaroslav Seifert. SNKHLU (State Publishing House of Literature, Music, and Art), Prague.

1961 • KARLUV MOST (Charles Bridge). Photographs by Josef Sudek, text by Emanuel Poche. SNKLHU (State Publishing House of Literature, Music, and Art), Prague.

1962 • JOSEF SUDEK PROFILY (Profiles). Edition of twelve postcards by Josef Sudek, text by Jan Rezac. Orbis, Prague.

1964 • SUDEK by Jan Rezac. Text in German, English, and French. Artia, Prague.

1969 • MOSTECKO-HUMBOLDTKA. Photographic panoramas by Josef Sudek. 2000 editions of eleven postcards. Dialog, Czechoslovakia.

1970 • WYCHOWANIE MUZYCZNE (A Musical Education). Photographs by Josef Sudek, text by Alojz Suchanek. Polish edition. Statni Pedagogicke Nakladatelstvi, Czechoslovakia.

1971 • JANACEK-HUKVALDY. Photographs by Josef Sudek, introduction by Jaroslav Seda. Text in Czech, German, and English. Supraphon, Czechoslovakia.

1976 • JOSEF SUDEK PORTFOLIO. 3,000 editions of thirteen original photographs (not printed by Sudek), introduction by Petr Tausk. Text in Czech, Russian, German, English, and French. Pressfoto, CTK, Prague.

ARTICLES AND PHOTOGRAPHS IN MAGAZINES, BOOKS, AND CATALOGS

Even though the following list is not complete, it is based upon information I have compiled from many diverse sources and represents what I believe is the most complete reference on Sudek to date. And, I apologize if inadvertently something is omitted.

MAGAZINES

1932 • ZIJEME (Cz.), "Fotograf Josef Sudek" by P. Altschul.

1955 • CESKOSLOVENSKA FOTOGRAFIE (Cz.), "Josef Sudek" by J. Jenicek.

1956 • CESKOSLOVENSKA FOTOGRAFIE (Cz.), "60 Years of Josef Sudek" by L. Linhart.

1956 • CESKOSLOVENSKA FOTOGRAFIE (Cz.), "Josef Sudek and Jaromir Funke" by L. Linhart.

1956 • ZPRAVODAJ (Cz.), fall-winter, article by Vaclav Sivko.

1956 • VYTVARNA PRACE (Cz.), #5, "Josef Sudek: 60 Years" by V. Jiru.

1957 • CESKOSLOVENSKA FOTOGRAFIE (Cz.), "Josef Sudek" by V. Jiru.

1957 • KULTURA (Cz.), #2, article by J. Krofta.

1957 • NOVY ZIVOT (Cz.), #4, article by J. Pecirka.

1958 • CESKOSLOVENSKA FOTOGRAFIE (Cz.), "Josef Sudek" by Vaclav Sivko.

1959 • KVETEN (Cz.), "A Moment with Mr. Sudek" by J. Bocek.

1961 • CESKOSLOVENSKA FOTOGRAFIE (Cz.), "Josef Sudek Artist of Merit."

1961 • FOTOGRAFIE (Cz.), #4, "An Artist-Photographer."

1963 • MLADY POLYGRAF (Cz.), #9, "The Photographer Josef Sudek" by R. Skopec.

1963 • CESKOSLOVENSKA FOTOGRAFIE (Cz.), articles by O. Chaloupka and J. Brok.

1965 • KULTURNI TVORBA (Cz.), #7, article by V. Zykmund.

1966 • CESKOSLOVENSKA FOTOGRAFIE (Cz.), "Echo of Sudek in the USA."

1966 • FOTOGRAFIE (Cz.), #1, "Sudek."

1966 • CESKOSLOVENSKA FOTOGRAFIE (Cz.), #2, "70 Years—
Josef Sudek."
1966 • CAMERA (Switz.), #3, "Sudek" by Allan Porter and
"Sudek" by Jan Rezac.
1967 • CESKOSLOVENSKA FOTOGRAFIE (Cz.), "Josef Sudek—
My Favorite Photographs."
1967 • CESKOSLOVENSKA FOTOGRAFIE (Cz.), article by
Petr Tausk.
1967 • CAMERA (Switz.) July, "Panoramas of the Czechoslovakian
Landscape—Josef Sudek" by Allan Porter.
1969 • INFINITY (U.S.A.), December, ". . . and there is music"
by Sonja Bullaty and "Josef Sudek" by James Sage.
1969 • VLASTA (Cz.), September, "The Atelier under Petrin
Tower" with a poem for Josef Sudek by Jaroslav Seifert.
1970 • FOTOPRISMA (Cz.), #4, "Josef Sudek (A True Classic of
Czech Photography)" by Petr Tausk.
1970 • LIFE (U.S.A.), May 29th, "Gallery: Josef Sudek—Poet of
Prague."
1971 • U.S. CAMERA ANNUAL (U.S.A.), "Sudek" by Sonja
Bullaty.
1971 • CESKOSLOVENSKA FOTOGRAFIE (Cz.), "Josef Sudek at
75" by J. Masin.
1971 • VYTVARNICTVO, FOTOGRAFIA, FILM (Cz.), "Josef
Sudek at 75" by Petr Tausk.
1971 • FOTO MAGAZIN (West Germany), #10, "Josef Sudek
(Bohemian Romantic, Old Master of Czechoslovak
Photography)" by Franz Pangerl.
1971 • FOTOGRAFIE (Cz.), #3, "Sudek at 75."
1972 • CAMERA (Switz.) #12, "Photographie 1839–1972."
1972 • THE PHOTOREPORTER, (U.S.A.), Vol. 2, "Josef Sudek's
American Bow" by Jacob Deschin.
1973 • FOTOGRAFIE (Cz.), #1, "Janacek-Hukvaldy" by J. Macku.
1973 • FOTOGRAFIE (Cz.), #2, "Josef Sudek" by V. Remes and
"Image Quality" by J. Andel.
1973 • VYTVARNICTVO, FOTOGRAFIA, FILM (Cz.), "Sudkove
Hukvaldy" by A. Dufek.
1974 • FOTOGRAFIA ITALIANA (Italy), #193, article by
Petr Tausk.
1974 • UMENI A REMESLA (Cz.), #2, article by Z. Kirschner.
1974 • POPULAR PHOTOGRAPHY (U.S.A.), November, article by
Paul Ginsberg.
1974 • LITERARNI MESICNIK (Cz.), April, "Josef Sudek: the
Man and the Photographer" by Daniela Mrazkova and
"Conversations with Sudek" by V. Kolar.
1974 • CESKOSLOVENSKA FOTOGRAFIE (Cz.), #2, "Josef
Sudek (Artist of Merit of Czechoslovakia)" by J. Andel.
1975 • CREATIVE CAMERA (Great Britain), October, "Josef
Sudek—The Birthplace of Janacek."
1976 • REVUE FOTOGRAFIE (Cz.), January, "The Photographer
and a Dream" by Kamil Lhotak and "Josef Sudek and His
Place In Czech Photography" by Jan Jedlan.
1976 • CAMERA (Switz.), #4, "Josef Sudek: A Monograph" with
articles by Allan Porter and Anna Farova.
1976 • CAMERA 35 (U.S.A.), "Mirror on Birthdays—Josef Sudek"
by Michael Edelson.
1976 • MODERN PHOTOGRAPHY (U.S.A.), September, "Josef
Sudek: The Czech Romantic" by Charles Sawyer.

1976 • THE BRITISH JOURNAL OF PHOTOGRAPHY (Great
Britain), December, "Josef Sudek—A Tribute to His Life
His Work" by Ruth Spencer.
1976 • KVETY (Cz.), "A Classic of Czech Photography" by
Hugo Schreiber.
1976 • DIKOBRAZ (Cz.), September 1, article by Jana Brabcova.
1977 • ZOOM (France), August-September, "Josef Sudek" by
Anna Farova.
1977 • THE PRINT COLLECTOR'S NEWSLETTER (U.S.A.),
Vol. VIII #4, "Josef Sudek: Photographs" by
Carter Ratcliffe.

BOOKS

1946 • PRAZSKE PALACE (Prague Palaces) by Alois Kubicek,
Prazske Nakladatelstvi V. Polacka v Praze (Prague
Publishing House of J. Prochazka, Prague).
1959 • LIGHT AND SHADOW, Artia, Prague.
1961 • PRAZSKE ATELIERY (Prague Ateliers), Nakladatelstvi
Ceskoslovenskych Vytvarnych Umelcu, Praha (Publishing
House of the Czechoslovak Graphic Artists, Prague).
1971 • GREAT PHOTOGRAPHERS, "Josef Sudek," Time/Life
Books, New York.
1975 • THE MAGIC IMAGE, Weidenfeld & Nicolson, London.
1977 • PHOTOGRAPHY YEAR/1976, "Josef Sudek—Poet of
Prague," Time/Life Books, New York.

CATALOGS OF SHOWS

1933 • Group show at Krasna Jizba, Prague.
1938 • Group show in Prague. Text by L. Linhart.
1958 • Show at Ales Hall, Artists Association, Prague.
Photographs 1955–1958. Text by Jan Rezac.
1960 • Show at Mlada Fronta, Prague. "Sudek in the Graphic Arts"
with introduction by Vaclav Sivko.
1961 • Group show in Prague. Text by R. Skopec.
1963 • Show in Prague. Text by Jan Rezac.
1964 • Show in Prague. Text by J. Lakosil.
1966 • Show in Prague. Text by K. Dvorak.
1967 • Shows in Prague-Brno. Text by Anna Farova.
1967 • Group show in Prague. "Czechoslovak Photography
between Two World Wars," text by R. Skopec.
1968 • Group show at Sheldon Memorial Art Gallery, University
of Nebraska, Lincoln, Nebraska. "Five Photographers."
1971 • Show in Brno. "Sudek Photographs 1950–1970, from the
Museum Collection."
1973 • Shows in Prague-Brno. Text by Anna Farova.
1976 • Show at Umeleckoprumyslove Muzeum (Museum of
Decorative Arts) in Prague for Sudek's 80th birthday.
"Sudek," text by Anna Farova. Published by Polygrafia 2,
Czechoslovakia.
1976 • Show in Brno, Moravia, for Sudek's 80th birthday. "Josef
Sudek," text in Czech and English by Antonin Dufek.
Published by Polygrafia, Czechoslovakia.
1976 • Show at Galerie Lichttropfen, Aachen, Germany. "Josef
Sudek," text by W. Lippert and Petr Tausk.
Edition Lichttropfen.

V I S I T S

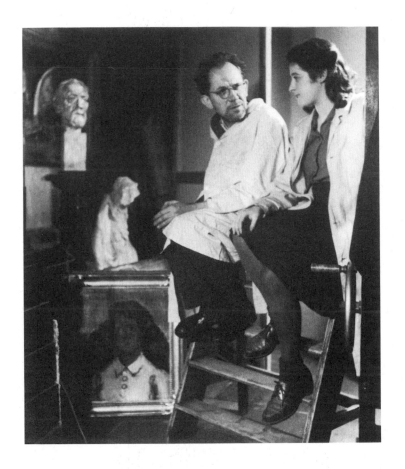

Self-portrait with Sudek, 1946, in the studio on Ujezd, made just before I left Czechoslovakia.

Sudek, 1960, at our first reunion in Prague after I left Czechoslovakia.

The studio in Uvoz, 1976.

On May 17, 1976 I took this last photograph of Sudek outside his studio; and it was the last time I saw him.